CLEOPATRA

CLEOPATRA

BY
ROBERT GREEN

A FIRST BOOK

FRANKLIN WATTS
A DIVISION OF GROLIER PUBLISHING
NEW YORK – LONDON – HONG KONG – SYDNEY
DANBURY, CONNECTICUT

For D.R. Green

Cover design by Robin Hoffmann
Cover photograph copyright ©: Art Resource, NY (Archivi Alinari)

Map by MacArt Design
Photographs copyright ©: Art Resource, NY: frontis (Archivi Alinari), pp. 21,
38, 44 (all Scala); The Bridgeman Library: pp. 36, 46; The Bettmann Archive:
pp. 8, 25, 28, 49, 52, 56; UPI/Bettmann: p. 29; Hulton Deutsh Collection: pp. 12
(both), 13, 16; North Wind Picture Archives: pp. 14, 31, 34, 40, 41, 54.

Library of Congress Cataloging-in-Publication Data

Green, Robert.
Cleopatra / by Robert Green.
p.   cm. — (A First book)
Includes bibliographial references and index.
Summary: Presents the life of the Egyptian queen whose dream of controlling
most of the known world was never fulfilled even though
she was allied to a powerful Roman.
ISBN 0-531-20231-3 (lib. bdg.)—ISBN 0-531-15800-4 (pbk.)
1. Cleopatra, Queen of Egypt, d. 30 B.C.—Juvenile literature.
2. Queens—Egypt—Biography—Juvenile literature.   [1. Cleopatra,
Queen of Egypt, d. 30 B.C.   2. Kings, queens, rulers, etc.]
I. Title.   II. Series.
DT92.7.G73   1996
932'.02'092—dc20   *95-43207 CIP AC*
[B]

CONTENTS

High-minded Cleopatra, that with stroke
Of asps' sting herself did stoutly kill
——EDMUND SPENSER, FROM THE FAERIE QUEENE

1

EGYPT OF THE PTOLEMIES

When Julius Caesar, Rome's most celebrated leader, landed in Egypt in 48 B.C., Egypt was in the midst of a civil war. A young king named Ptolemy XIII was competing against his twenty-year-old sister, Cleopatra, for power in Egypt. Caesar moved into the royal palace of Egypt's capital city, Alexandria, where he found himself surrounded by Ptolemy's soldiers. Upon hearing of Caesar's arrival, Cleopatra sped to Alexandria to ask for his support. To enter the palace undetected, Cleopatra rolled herself up in a carpet. Her servant Apollodorus draped the carpet over his shoulder and carried it boldly past the palace guards. Apollodorus presented the carpet to Caesar as a present from

Cleopatra. To Caesar's delight, out came the slender queen.

The manner in which Cleopatra presented herself to Caesar tells us much about Cleopatra's character. She was bold and clever, and she had flair. Cleopatra spoke to Caesar in Latin, the language of the Romans, and her words charmed him. Even though she was only twenty, Cleopatra impressed Caesar with her courage, her marvelous stories, and her proud ways. When Caesar arrived in Egypt, Cleopatra was not well known outside Egypt. When Caesar left Egypt, Cleopatra was seated firmly on the Egyptian throne. She was also pregnant with Caesar's son.

Cleopatra knew that, in a world controlled by Rome, she would have to ally herself to a powerful Roman leader to become a great queen. She first allied herself with Caesar, and profited from this connection, but he was already quite old. She was then able to win the affection of Marc Antony, one of Caesar's successors. She took a gamble, and she used all her courage and charm and the wealth of Egypt, to build a vast empire. The story of Antony and

Cleopatra unfurls herself from a carpet after being secreted into the royal palace at Alexandria by her servant Apollodorus. Caesar, on the left, is delighted by the queen's entrance.

Cleopatra's bid for glory is one of the greatest stories of the ancient world. It affected not only Egypt and Rome but all the lands around the Mediterranean Sea.

EGYPT UNDER GREEK RULE

By the time of Cleopatra's birth in 69 B.C., Egypt had already been ruled by a foreign power, Greece, for more than 250 years. Greece preceded Rome in creating a vast empire in the lands surrounding the Mediterranean Sea and to the east. Egypt's ancient civilization had existed for thousands of years on its own, but then Alexander the Great, Greece's most celebrated leader, conquered it in 332 B.C.

To conquer Egypt, Alexander marched his armies across the Sinai Peninsula, which forms a land bridge between Asia and Africa. This is a torturous route, made mostly of desert sands and rocky hills that provide little shelter or water. Alexander dreamed of a port city in Egypt where the trade caravans from the east could meet the ships of the Mediterranean.

To build his new port city, Alexander chose a limestone peninsula jutting into the sea near the western-most side of the Nile Delta. He called the new city Alexandria, in honor of himself. Having no other material at hand, he marked the boundaries of the city wall with grain from his soldiers' food supplies.

ALEXANDER'S LEGACY

When Alexander died, in 323 B.C., the Greek empire was divided among three families. One of the three, the Ptolemies, ruled Egypt from Alexandria. The main language and culture in Alexandria was Greek, but every manner of Mediterranean peoples could be found combing the streets of the city. Ships from countries all around the Mediterranean Sea could be seen in the great harbor.

In the middle of Alexandria's harbor stood one of the wonders of the ancient world—a towering lighthouse built on the island of Pharos. Ancient artists portrayed this lighthouse soaring above the city and spitting flames into the surrounding sky. The fire that burned in the lighthouse was magnified by a series of mirrors, giving it a splendid brightness. Sailors could use it to chart their course to Alexandria, which had, as Alexander hoped, become a magnificent trading center.

By Cleopatra's time Alexandria had become a truly international city. It was divided into three main districts: the Jewish quarter, the Rhacotis (Egyptian quarter), and the Brucheum (Royal Greek quarter). Most of the activity of the city centered around its harbor.

Alexandria also became a center of arts and

The great lighthouse on the island of Pharos in Alexandria's harbor was designed by the Greek architect Sostratos during the reign of King Ptolemy II. Over centuries, earthquakes, fires, and wars destroyed the lighthouse, and today most of the island of Pharos is underwater.

PHAROS

As these three pictures demonstrate, artists have had different conceptions of what the lighthouse looked like. Estimates of its height range from 200 to 600 feet (60 to 180 meters). Descriptions and stories of the ancient world have often been exaggerated in retellings. Many times they reflect the tastes of the era in which the story or painting was produced rather than the authentic historical event.

learning. The first Ptolemy constructed a library and a museum in Alexandria and invited foreign scholars to make use of them. By Cleopatra's time, the library at Alexandria held over 700,000 volumes in many languages, such as Greek, Latin, Hebrew, and Aramaic. It was the most extensive collection of learning anywhere in the ancient world. Ptolemy I also constructed a sumptuous palace for the Ptolemaic rulers. He erected temples and monuments to various gods, both Greek and Egyptian.

Cleopatra was descended from the first Ptolemy. It was the custom of the Ptolemies to marry their relatives to keep the family lineage Greek. Because of this practice, Cleopatra was not really Egyptian. She was solely of Greek descent. She was a foreign queen, the successor to a dynasty left from the days of Greek supremacy in the ancient world. But when Cleopatra ruled Egypt from 51 B.C. to 30 B.C., Egypt lived in the shadow of Rome. Rome had followed Greece as the greatest power of the Mediterranean world.

The great Alexandrian Library;
in Cleopatra's time, this library was
by far the largest in the world. It was
one of the reasons Alexandria was a
center of learning.

The Greek rulers of Egypt, although fiercely proud of their own traditions, could not help comparing themselves to the pharaohs of more ancient days. This picture shows a bust of Ptolemy Auletes, Cleopatra's father, in the rigid artistic style of pharaonic Egypt. Egyptians, however, could never get over the fact that their new rulers were foreigners, and the Ptolemies never reached the greatness of their predecessors.

Yet Cleopatra would not let Roman power go unchallenged. She remembered the greatness of her Greek ancestors. She remembered the splendor of the ancient Egyptian pharaohs, whose lands she now ruled. She determined to make a bid for power, hurling herself into the heart of Roman politics. In 1845 the French poet Theophile Gautier was thinking of her determination and recklessness when he wrote that Cleopatra "is a person to be wondered at . . . whom dreamers find always at the end of their dreams."

2

EGYPT AND ROME

like a vast web, the Roman world stretched from Britain to North Africa and from Spain to the border of Asia. Rome, at the center of this web, demanded gold, silver, jewels, spices, livestock, and other goods from all its provinces. The Romans considered Rome to be the center of the world. In many ways, it was. They did not know about distant lands such as China or the Americas, but they conquered almost all the countries they could reach.

Rome's government was based on an unwritten constitution and a group of lawmakers called senators. Two men, called *consuls*, oversaw the republic. This system was intended to prevent any one man from gaining too much power.

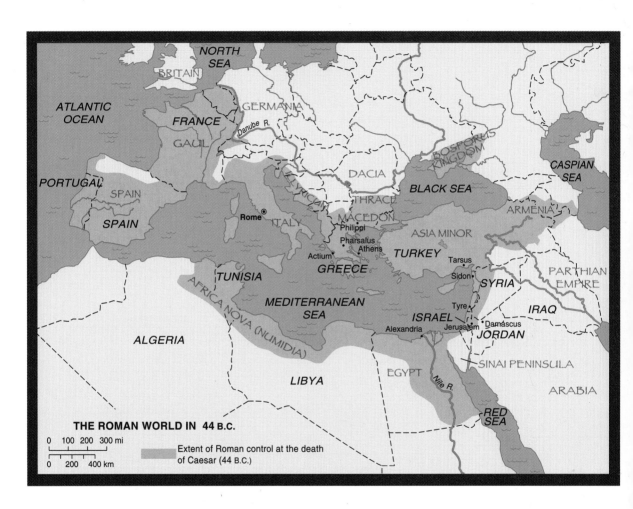

THE ROMAN WORLD IN 44 B.C.

0 100 200 300 mi

0 200 400 km

Extent of Roman control at the death
of Caesar (44 B.C.)

Labels on map:

NORTH SEA
BRITAIN
ATLANTIC OCEAN
GERMANIA
FRANCE
GAUL
Danube R.
DACIA
BOSPORUS KINGDOM
CASPIAN SEA
BLACK SEA
THRACE
ARMENIA
PORTUGAL
SPAIN
SPAIN
ILLYRICUM
Rome
ITALY
MACEDON
Philippi
Pharsalus
ASIA MINOR
Athens
TURKEY
PARTHIAN EMPIRE
Actium
GREECE
Tarsus
Sidon
SYRIA
IRAQ
TUNISIA
MEDITERRANEAN SEA
Tyre
ISRAEL
Damascus
JORDAN
ALGERIA
AFRICA NOVA (NUMIDIA)
Alexandria
Jerusalem
SINAI PENINSULA
ARABIA
LIBYA
EGYPT
Nile R.
RED SEA

By Caesar's time, however, the government had become corrupt. People were losing faith in these leaders. Romans still feared the rise of a tyrant. Even so, Caesar himself had long been building his own base of political power, personal wealth, and military strength. He was planning to become the single most powerful man in Rome.

THE FIRST TRIUMVIRATE

In 60 B.C. (when Cleopatra was nine), Julius Caesar, Crassus, and Pompey formed a Triumvirate, or a government of three, to ensure a balance of power. The Roman provinces were divided into three parts, each of which would be ruled by a Triumvir.

Ptolemy Auletes, who was Cleopatra's father, had appealed to the Triumvirate of Rome. He was a cruel,

The Senate was the backbone of the Roman Republic, but senators grew more and more greedy for power and privileges, so the people looked elsewhere for leadership. In this painting, Cicero, one of the greatest of all Roman orators, denounces a political opponent in the Roman Senate. Caesar, after becoming dictator, greatly diminished the powers of the Senate.

greedy, and corrupt leader. Upon finding a revolt brewing in his empire, Ptolemy begged the Triumvirs to intervene on his behalf. Pompey was campaigning in the east, but Julius Caesar and Crassus publicly supported Ptolemy. Then they demanded that he pay them a vast sum of money.

The Egyptians resented the poor bargain Ptolemy Auletes had made with Rome. Matters worsened for Ptolemy until he was forced to flee the open violence of Alexandria. He returned to Rome and asked for help in crushing the revolt. The Romans restored Ptolemy Auletes to power by force. Now Rome had entered directly into Egyptian affairs.

CIVIL WARS IN EGYPT AND ROME

Upon returning to power with the help of Rome, Ptolemy Auletes had Cleopatra marry Ptolemy XIII, one of her brothers. It was the practice of the Ptolemies, like the Egyptian pharaohs before them, to marry brother to sister to retain the royal lineage. At the time, Cleopatra was seventeen years old and her brother was ten. Jealousies quickly sprang up between Cleopatra and Ptolemy XIII, who was under the guidance of an adviser named Pothinus. Their jealousies led to open war. Meanwhile Rome was plunged into civil war as well.

The Roman Civil War was set off when Crassus

was slain while waging a battle in the east against Parthia (roughly modern Iran). The death of Crassus brought the end of the first Triumvirate. Civil war soon broke out between the surviving Triumvirs, Caesar and Pompey. Pompey spoke against Caesar in the Roman Senate, while Caesar marched toward Rome to meet Pompey's challenge. Caesar wrenched Italy from Pompey's grasp, then pursued him to central Greece, where the decisive battle of the Civil War was fought. Caesar overwhelmed Pompey's forces in the battle of Pharsalus in 48 B.C.

Pompey escaped to Egypt, where he hoped to receive help from the Ptolemies. News of Caesar's victory, however, had already reached Egypt. Pothinus, who was ruling in the king's name, joined a plot against Pompey. Pompey's head was cut off as soon as he landed in Egypt.

CAESAR SIDES WITH CLEOPATRA

Four days later, when Caesar landed in Egypt, he was presented with Pompey's head. Pompey had been Caesar's archenemy, but the sight of the tattered, severed head of this once-triumphant champion of Rome disgusted Caesar. Caesar now despised Ptolemy XIII and Pothinus for taking the head of Pompey. He became a supporter of Cleopatra in the Egyptian civil war. Relations between Cleopatra and her brother, who was under the guidance of Pothinus, had quickly deteriorated. By the time Caesar landed in Egypt, both factions had amassed troops of Greek soldiers and mercenaries. Most Egyptians were probably resentful of both sides and indifferent to the outcome of the war. Chaos, however, erupted in Alexandria and there was a great deal of random violence.

By the time Cleopatra had been smuggled in a rug into the palace to see Caesar, he was already involved in the Egyptian civil war. Caesar's forces were few and weary from pursuit of Pompey, but he wanted to help Cleopatra. Caesar sent for reinforcements from the Roman province of Syria, and then prepared to wait with Cleopatra.

Ptolemy XIII and Pothinus were also living in the same palace. Pothinus secretly stirred up much trouble for Caesar while openly pretending to be his

A statue of Julius Caesar as a younger man—with a full head of hair. By the time Caesar reached Alexandria in 48 B.C., his forehead was much higher. Cleopatra, who wrote a book on cosmetics (which has since been lost), may have offered Caesar remedies to apply to his bald patches. The ingredients of Cleopatra's hair tonic included burnt mice and horse teeth.

friend. On hearing of Pothinus's intrigues, Caesar had him put to death. Once Pothinus was dead, Ptolemy XIII could see how taken Caesar was with Cleopatra. Ptolemy threw down his crown, fled the palace, and joined the forces against Caesar.

While Caesar awaited reinforcements from Syria, he set fire to ships anchored in the harbor at Alexandria. He feared that his enemies would use the ships to attack him. Legend has it that some of the ships drifted to the shore, spreading fire to the great library of Alexandria and destroying many precious books. But this may have been a rumor started by Pompey's followers to discredit Caesar.

When Caesar's reinforcements finally arrived from Syria, the Egyptians suffered many losses. They surrendered, and Caesar was triumphant. After one battle, the lifeless body of Ptolemy XIII was found in the Nile River, his golden armor still glittering through the water. Caesar called this conflict in Egypt the Alexandrine War. Caesar and Cleopatra were its victors.

3

UPHEAVAL IN ROME

To celebrate their victory in the Alexandrine War, Caesar and Cleopatra took a pleasure cruise up the Nile River in a magnificent barge. They watched entertainments and feasted. Caesar marveled at the many ancient temples and monuments along the Nile's banks.

Meanwhile, matters in Rome were still in turmoil from the Civil War. Some of the Roman provinces were rebelling. Finally, Caesar tore himself from the pleasures of Cleopatra's court. But before leaving Egypt, he married Cleopatra to her eleven-year-old brother, Ptolemy XIV, and placed both of them on the throne, as was the tradition of the Ptolemies.

Cleopatra was very rich and given to extravagance. Slaves hurried about her court obeying her every demand, while asses' milk, which filled her lavish tub, softened her skin. After the Alexandrine War, Caesar and Cleopatra took a pleasure cruise down the Nile to see the splendid monuments and ruins along the river's banks.

Actress Elizabeth Taylor in the title role of the 1963 movie Cleopatra. *Cleopatra visited Rome while Caesar was at the height of his power. The Roman people received Cleopatra with pomp and splendor. Even though Caesar did not acknowledge Caesarion as his son, as Cleopatra was hoping, his continued affection for Cleopatra caused many Romans to turn against him.*

Ptolemy XIV had no Pothinus to guide him. The real power was now in the hands of Cleopatra. Caesar spent the next year in foreign campaigns, quieting the provinces, before returning to Rome.

THE IDES OF MARCH

While Caesar was engaged in his foreign campaigns, stories of his life of pleasure with Cleopatra reached Rome. He lost much favor with the Romans, who questioned the wisdom of lying idle for such an extended time and making a mistress of a foreign queen. The Romans also heard about Caesar's son by Cleopatra. He had been named Ptolemy XV Caesar, but was commonly known as Caesarion. Calpurnia, Caesar's wife, suffered from this news. A group of conspirators in Rome, led by Brutus and Cassius, began plotting the murder of Caesar.

Despite all the resentment against Caesar, he was still greeted as a conqueror when he returned to Rome in 46 B.C. Four splendid processions, one to celebrate each of his major conquests, heralded his return. Trumpets sounded, gladiators clashed, and exotic animals panted and snorted in the streets. Even a replica of the lighthouse at Pharos rolled through Rome, spitting flame and smoke. Caesar's enemies watched patiently.

Cleopatra arrived in Rome with Caesarion at

To rid Rome of its dictator and to save
their own power as senators, Cassius,
Brutus, and their fellow conspirators killed
Caesar on the floor of the Senate in 44 B.C.

about this time. She was welcomed as a royal visitor to Caesar's house. Caesar would not publicly recognize Caesarion as his son, however. He knew that doing so would enrage the Romans, who were generally sympathetic to Calpurnia. Caesar found other ways, however, of honoring Cleopatra. He dedicated a new temple, called Venus Genetrix, to Cleopatra. He also had a statue cast in the likeness of Cleopatra to represent the Roman goddess Venus.

All this was just too much for the Romans. They speculated wildly about what Caesar might do next. Some feared that he would rule the Roman world from Alexandria with Cleopatra as his queen. Talk of assassinating him flew throughout the city. Bad dreams plagued Calpurnia, and oracles prophesied doom for Caesar. Finally, on March 15, 44 B.C.—the "Ides of March"—Brutus, Cassius, and others set upon Caesar in the Senate and stabbed him to death.

OCTAVIUS AND ANTONY

After the assassination, two camps emerged. There were those who supported the assassins Brutus and Cassius, and others who sought to avenge Caesar's death. Public opinion turned strongly against Caesar's assassins, so Brutus and Cassius fled. Those loyal to Caesar rallied around two figures—Octavius, Caesar's adopted son, and Marc Antony, the highest-ranking official in Rome at the time of Caesar's death. Both men were striking figures. Both had been favorites of Caesar.

Marc Antony claimed that he was descended from the powerful Hercules, a hero of Greek and Roman mythology. He grew his hair and beard long and wore a thick cloak resembling Hercules's lion skin. Antony was courageous, like Hercules, and his soldiers loved him. But he could also be boastful and reckless.

Octavius was very nearly Antony's opposite. His thin body was usually draped in expensive robes, and his manners and tastes were refined. Antony had won his reputation through war. Octavius had won his through politics and oratory (the art of public speaking). Whereas Antony could be reckless, Octavius was always restrained. The differences between Antony and Octavius would greatly affect the future of Rome, but for the present, they joined together to avenge the death of Caesar.

Octavius and Antony formed the second Triumvirate with a military officer named Lepidus. Then Octavius and Antony set out after Brutus and Cassius, who had moved their armies eastward.

While the supporters of Caesar gave chase to Brutus and Cassius, Cleopatra watched anxiously, waiting for a victor to emerge. At Philippi, in 42 B.C., Octavius and Antony met the armies of Brutus and

After Caesar's murder, an eerie quiet descended on Rome. Then Marc Antony addressed the Roman people, with Caesar's body on display, and called for revenge against the conspirators.

Cassius and won a decisive battle. Knowing that all was lost for them, Brutus and Cassius committed suicide.

When Antony and Octavius returned triumphant, they suspected Lepidus of treachery. They swept him aside and divided the Roman provinces between themselves. Provinces in the west went to Octavius, and the eastern provinces went to Antony. At the time of his assassination, Caesar had been planning an expedition eastward to destroy the Parthians. Their defeat of Crassus some time earlier had been a lasting insult to Rome. Antony now made this ambition his own and sailed east.

CLEOPATRA'S HELP

Having few resources to fund such a campaign, Antony appealed to Cleopatra for support. He summoned Cleopatra to his camp at Tarsus on the shores of southern Turkey. Cleopatra knew that she must win Antony to her side, for she needed the support of Rome to enlarge her own power. She decided to use all her charm and wealth to win him over. She set out on a splendid barge, dressed as Venus, the Roman goddess of love. She was attended by beautiful children draped in jewels, who appeared in various likenesses of Cupid—the child of Venus. Splendid purple sails captured the wind. Silver oars lapped the sea to

When Antony summoned Cleopatra to a meeting at the port city of Tarsus, Cleopatra won his support and his heart as well. Cleopatra was dressed as Venus, the Roman goddess of love. She was surrounded by the melodies of flutes and harps, the scent of flowers and perfumes. Antony was enchanted.

the rhythm of drums, flutes, and harps. Around the barge hung the many scents of Egypt's perfumes.

When Cleopatra landed at Tarsus, the townspeople gazed with open mouths at the queen's splendor. The proud Antony, who had not come to greet her, summoned her to a banquet. Cleopatra declined, bidding Antony to her. She was determined to present herself as Antony's equal. Antony gave in. For two nights he feasted at her splendid banquets and listened as stories floated from her clever tongue. He marveled at her gold and silver plates and cups, studded with colored jewels. These Cleopatra distributed to the guests as they left the banquet. On the second night, even more splendid objects filled the room. These Cleopatra gave to Antony after the feast.

Cleopatra's charms were not wasted; Antony was wildly attracted to her. He put off all plans for attacking the Parthians and accompanied Cleopatra to Alexandria. Antony followed Caesar in taking Cleopatra for a mistress. This began a powerful alliance that would threaten Octavius and once again plunge Rome into civil war.

This painting depicts the legendary account of Cleopatra dissolving one of her largest and most lustrous pearls into a glass of vinegar, which she then drank, to the astonishment of her guests. The incident reflects not only her interest in cosmetics (the mixture was supposed to be good for the complexion), but also her tendency to flaunt her wealth.

4

ANTONY AND CLEOPATRA

Alexandria suited Antony. He fell easily into the Greek ways of Cleopatra's court. Unlike Caesar, Antony made it known that he was a guest of the queen and not a conqueror. He spoke Greek and wore Greek clothing. Though an able politician and a valiant general, Antony had a weakness for luxury and games. It was his habit to go into the streets of Alexandria disguised as a commoner in order to eat, drink, and joke with the Alexandrians. The people saw through his disguises but liked him all the more for his simplicity and goodwill.

While Antony lingered in Egypt in 41 B.C., his enemies were on the move elsewhere. The Parthians

invaded eastern Roman provinces, sweeping through Asia Minor (modern Turkey) and Syria. By the time news of this reached Antony, Roman soldiers had already joined the side of the Parthians in Syria. In Rome, Antony's affairs also grew worse. Fulvia, Antony's wife, and Lucius Antonius, Antony's brother, rebelled against Octavius in Antony's name. By

Before the Nile was dammed at Aswan in 1968, it rose and fell once a year, leaving dark, fertile soil along its banks. Egyptian farmers, called fellahin, reaped enormous food crops from the Nile's banks, and Egypt became the granary to the Mediterranean world. Cleopatra, pictured here sailing up the Cydnus (the modern Tarsus) River in southern Turkey, supported her extravagance and her military adventures by driving a hard bargain. She sold grain in times of famine at high prices and leased Egyptian land holdings in Judea (modern Israel) at an exorbitant rate to King Herod for his fruit crops.

attacking Octavius, Fulvia hoped to draw Antony away from Cleopatra. Instead, Octavius crushed the rebellion and drove Fulvia into Greece.

Hearing of this turn of events, Antony sailed east and hastily attempted to strengthen his defenses against the Parthians. Then he departed for Athens, where Fulvia awaited him. In Athens, Antony brooded over his future, while Fulvia became ill. She had succeeded in drawing Antony away from Cleopatra, but she died only a short time later.

CLEOPATRA WITHOUT ANTONY

Antony headed for Rome, where he blamed the plot against Octavius on the recently deceased Fulvia. Octavius accepted the explanation, and in 40 B.C. the two entered into a new alliance. They sealed it by marrying Octavius's sister Octavia to Antony. News of Antony's new marriage reached Cleopatra just weeks after she had given birth to Antony's twin children, whom she named Alexander Helios and Cleopatra Selene. Cleopatra's hopes were dashed. Antony now had a new wife and new obligations in Rome.

For three and a half years (40–36 B.C.), Cleopatra and Antony were separated. Cleopatra turned to matters of state, making alliances and trade agreements with surrounding countries and providing for Egyptians who could not grow food during a drought. Cleopatra was a shrewd leader and a hard bargainer. Her wealth grew, and with it she built warships and filled the ranks of her army.

Antony, too, prepared for war. He was still popular with the Roman people and used his influence to build an army that could, once and for all, destroy the Parthians. He gave Octavius ships in exchange for foot soldiers and appealed to Cleopatra to fund the expedition. Meanwhile, his power grew steadily in Rome. Even so, he knew he needed victory over the Parthians to keep Octavius from winning the Romans to his side.

Antony intended to march through Asia Minor and Armenia and attack the Parthians from the north. The Greek historian Plutarch wrote that all his preparations "terrified even the Indians and made all Asia afraid." But Antony was too impatient. He sent his light troops ahead of the supplies and reserves. The Parthians seized the opportunity to destroy Antony's supply train and slaughter his rear guard. As a result, the Romans began to starve early in their campaign.

Antony was forced to ask the Parthians for a peaceful retreat. The Parthians agreed. Then they violated that bargain and set upon the retreating Romans, killing them off in lightning raids. Antony lost many more men to the frigid winds and heavy snows of winter. Cleopatra sailed for the port city of Sidon on the eastern Mediterranean coast with relief supplies for Antony. Upon seeing the condition of Antony's army, which was reduced to a fraction of its original size, her heart must have sunk.

MVNIF.PL.IX.P.M.
AN.XVIII

OCTAVIA ABANDONED

Antony sailed to Alexandria with Cleopatra, where he could recuperate in the luxury of her court. Antony's wife, Octavia, however, had not forsaken him. She was said to possess "beauty, honor, and prudence." But of all her qualities, devotion took the highest place. When she heard of Antony's defeat by the Parthians, she collected men and supplies for Antony and traveled to Greece to meet him. Antony accepted her supplies, but he refused to see her, sailing back to Egypt and Cleopatra. This was just one more insult to his wife and to Octavius. In fact, Octavius may have allowed the meeting to take place just so Antony could insult Octavia. If it was a trick, it worked. Octavius began preparing for war against Antony and Cleopatra.

Antony put the supplies he received from Octavia to good use in attacking the Armenians, who had joined the Parthians against him. In 34 B.C. Antony's forces defeated the Armenians and captured their king. Antony celebrated the victory with a Triumph. A Triumph was a formal celebration of a military vic-

After years of struggle against Marc Antony for power, Octavius took on the title Augustus Caesar, first Emperor of Rome, in 27 B.C.

Cleopatra was said to have an allure that distracted
Marc Antony from his obligations to Rome.

tory. As the main event of the Triumph, Antony led the Armenian king through the streets of Alexandria in golden chains. By Roman custom, a leader could celebrate a victory with a Triumph only if it had been approved by the Roman Senate. It also had to be celebrated in Rome. Antony ignored this custom by holding his in Alexandria.

Antony's Triumph generated much resentment toward him in Rome. The Romans could clearly see that he preferred Alexandria to his native city. Every move Antony made was bringing him closer to war with Octavius.

5

ACTIUM AND AFTER

In a stadium just outside Alexandria, Antony and Cleopatra hosted a great gathering of Alexandrians in a ceremony known as the Donations of Alexandria. Seated on thrones of solid gold, they ladled honors and titles upon themselves. Antony was dressed as the Greek god Dionysus, and Cleopatra was dressed as the Egyptian goddess Isis. They proclaimed themselves sole rulers of the eastern Roman provinces and proclaimed Alexandria their capital. During the festivities, Antony sacrificed to the eastern god Serapis, rather than to the Roman god Jupiter. He did not seem to care that such an act would be considered a sacrilege by the Romans.

Cleopatra is pictured in this relief sculpture as the Egyptian goddess Isis. Egyptian and Roman leaders portrayed themselves in the likenesses of gods or goddesses in attempts to appear larger than life. Often such self-promotion had political aims as well. Even though it insulted the Romans, Antony paid reverence to Egyptian rather than Roman gods; he was showing his allegiance to Cleopatra and Egypt.

Antony publicly recognized Cleopatra as his wife and honored his children by her. He gave each of them rule of lesser kingdoms in the east. Antony also honored the son of Caesar and Cleopatra, Caesarion. He crowned Caesarion "King of Kings," and heir to all the Roman provinces. It must be remembered that Octavius was Caesar's stepson. By recognizing Caesarion as Caesar's sole heir, Antony was directly challenging Octavius's right to rule the provinces and Rome itself.

OCTAVIUS'S CHALLENGE

Upon hearing of the Donations of Alexandria, Octavius spoke out against Antony in the Roman Senate. He accused Antony of preferring a foreign queen to his Roman wife and of preferring Alexandria to Rome. Moreover, Octavius said that Antony was giving away Roman provinces to foreigners and was threatening Rome by recognizing Caesar's illegitimate son Caesarion.

Octavius's words ignited the senators' fury. Then, to close his arguments, Octavius read Antony's will in the Senate. The will declared that, should Antony die in Rome, his body was to be taken to Cleopatra for burial in Egypt. The Senate erupted with resentment.

For the next few months, Octavius and Antony

prepared for war. Octavius moved first, declaring war on Cleopatra. He received the support of the Roman Senate. More important, he gave command of his fleet to a skilled naval commander named Marcus Agrippa.

BATTLE AT SEA

The opposing forces met at the peninsula of Actium in Greece in 31 B.C. Antony had more soldiers. Octavius was stronger at sea. Antony tried to pull Octavius into a land battle, but Octavius wisely resisted. Finally, urged by Cleopatra, the Battle of Actium was fought on September 2, 31 B.C., at sea. Antony's forces held at first, but Octavius's lighter ships, under the command of Agrippa, started to get the upper hand. In the middle of the battle Antony beheld an unbelievable sight. Cleopatra's flagship hoisted sail and fled. Antony chased after her, abandoning his fleet and his chances of victory. Left without a commander, Antony's naval officers surrendered to Octavius. Soon after, Antony's army also surrendered. The great battle that would determine who would control Rome and what would happen to Egypt was over. Antony and Cleopatra had lost.

Historians still argue over Cleopatra's motivation for abandoning the battle at Actium. Was it just cowardice? Was she trying to save the vast treasure

stored in the hold of her flagship? We may never know why she turned. We do know, however, that when she fled and Antony followed, their dreams of glory came to an end.

Antony and Cleopatra sailed to Egypt in brooding silence. The eastern kings, who had once been loyal to them, were rapidly going over to Octavius. After reaching Alexandria, Cleopatra ordered that Egypt's treasure be moved to a magnificent temple she had built for her entombment. She locked herself and two handmaidens inside. As a last resort, Cleopatra prepared to destroy the treasure and commit suicide. Antony, meanwhile, prepared his forces for another battle with Octavius, who was sailing toward Egypt in pursuit. Antony still commanded a small navy and

Marcus Agrippa rose from humble origins to become Augustus's chief military officer. The military provided one of the few opportunities for a man to rise above his station in the rigid Roman class system. Octavius, as Augustus Ceasar, rewarded Agrippa for his military victories, such as Actium, with three consulships and his daughter's hand in marriage.

It will never be known what made Cleopatra raise her sails and flee for home in the middle of the sea fight off the coast of Actium, but when Antony followed, leaving his navy without its leader, the battle was lost.

some foot soldiers. This time he was fighting only for his life.

THE END OF A DREAM

When Octavius reached Egypt in August, 30 B.C., the Egyptian navy promptly surrendered in the harbor of Alexandria. In desperation, Antony and Cleopatra sent messages to Octavius. Cleopatra offered to surrender if Octavius would recognize Caesarion as ruler of Egypt. Antony promised a peaceful retirement if Octavius would spare his life. Octavius ignored their appeals and marched on Alexandria.

At Alexandria, Octavius's forces were momentarily beaten back by Antony's guard. But when a rumor that Cleopatra was dead reached Antony, he threw himself on his sword. He did not die instantly. Cleopatra ordered him to be carried into her temple, where he died in her arms.

Octavius feared that Cleopatra, too, would kill herself. He ordered his soldiers to enter the temple and capture her alive. When she caught sight of the intruders, she tried to thrust a knife into her breast, but the guards disarmed her. The historian Plutarch claimed that Octavius kept his eyes on the floor when he went to see Cleopatra. He wanted to avoid being attracted to the woman who had ruined Antony. His

The legendary death of Cleopatra by poisonous snake bite has sparked the imagination of artists throughout the ages.

guards managed to keep her from stabbing herself, but she found another way to die.

THE DEATH OF A QUEEN

According to Plutarch, she was brought a large basket of figs. It was a basket large enough to hold a snake. Soon after, she was found dead. Two red spots marked her arm, and the path of a snake was found in the sand nearby. Cleopatra had once made a study of poisons by feeding them to her slaves and watching the effects. She discovered that the bite of an asp, a snake found in Egypt, caused a short period of sleep and an apparently painless death.

Octavius never knew whether an asp or some other deadly means ended Cleopatra's life. He allowed Cleopatra and Antony to be buried together in Egypt, but he put Caesarion to death. Octavius annexed Egypt and in 27 B.C. declared himself Augustus Caesar, first Emperor of the Roman Empire.

Cleopatra died at the age of thirty-nine. She had ruled Egypt for twenty-two years. She was the last of the Ptolemies. Her death ended the Greek influence in Egypt, which had lasted for over three hundred years. She was a woman in a time when women were secondary to men. And she was a queen when queens were secondary to kings. But she dreamed of controlling most of the world that was known at the time, and she failed. Even though she was allied to a powerful Roman, she could not defeat Rome.

After the death of the historical Cleopatra, the Cleopatra of myth was born. Early historians told of her charms, wealth, and cruelty (she is said to have enjoyed sticking golden pins into her slaves). Shakespeare wrote of her, and fashionable European women copied her style. Film studios made movies about her. She captivated Julius Caesar in 48 B.C. and she still fascinates today, making her one of the most celebrated women of history.

TIMELINE

332 B.C.	Alexander the Great conquers Egypt
323 B.C.	Alexander dies; beginning of Ptolemaic rule in Egypt
69 B.C.	Cleopatra born
60 B.C.	Rome's first Triumvirate formed by Caesar, Crassus, and Pompey
58 B.C.	Ptolemy Auletes, Cleopatra's father, expelled from Egypt
55 B.C.	Rome restores Ptolemy to Egypt's throne by force; Cleopatra married to brother, Ptolemy XIII
53 B.C.	Civil war in Rome and Egypt
51 B.C.	Ptolemy Auletes dies, Cleopatra begins co-rule of Egypt with brother, Ptolemy XIII
48 B.C.	Caesar defeats Pompey at Pharsalus, arrives in Egypt, meets Cleopatra
47 B.C.	Caesar defeats Ptolemy XIII to end Egyptian civil war, Cleopatra and Ptolemy XIV placed on the throne by Caesar; Caesarion born
46–44 B.C.	Cleopatra visits Rome as Caesar's guest
44 B.C.	(March 15) The Ides of March—Caesar assassinated; Cleopatra returns to Egypt
42 B.C.	Octavius and Antony defeat Brutus and Cassius at Philippi
41 B.C.	Cleopatra goes to Tarsus to seek Antony's help
40–37 B.C.	Cleopatra and Antony separated (Antony in Rome, then Parthia)
37 B.C.	Cleopatra joins Antony in Sidon
34 B.C.	Antony defeats Armenians, celebrates with Triumph in Alexandria
32 B.C.	Octavius condemns Antony in Roman Senate; Rome declares war on Cleopatra
31 B.C.	Battle at Actium
30 B.C.	Egyptian navy surrenders to Octavius; Antony and Cleopatra commit suicide; Caesarion is murdered on Octavius's order
27 B.C.	Octavius annexes Egypt, declares himself Augustus Caesar, first Roman emperor

FOR MORE INFORMATION

FOR FURTHER READING

Corbishley, Mike. *Everyday Life in Roman Times*. New York: Franklin
 Watts, 1994.
Pearson, Anne. *Everyday Life in Ancient Egypt*. New York: Franklin Watts,
 1994.
Stanley, Diane, and Peter Vennema. *Cleopatra*. New York: Morrow Junior
 Books, 1994.

FOR ADVANCED READERS

Bradford, Ernle. *Cleopatra*. New York: Harcourt Brace Jovanovich, 1972.
Hughes-Hallett, Lucy. *Cleopatra: Histories, Dreams, and Distortions*. New
 York: HarperCollins, 1991.

FAMOUS RETELLINGS OF
CLEOPATRA'S STORY

Shakespeare, William. *Antony and Cleopatra*. This play has been done in
 two movie versions, one directed by Charlton Heston in 1973, the
 other a filmed stage production directed by Lawrence Carra in
 1981.

Shaw, George Bernard. *Caesar and Cleopatra*. This was also made into a
  movie in 1946, directed by Gabriel Pascal and starring Claude Rains
  and Vivien Leigh.
Cleopatra. Two famous movie versions. One was directed by Cecil B.
  DeMille in 1934. The other, directed by Joseph Mankiewicz in 1963,
  starred Elizabeth Taylor and Richard Burton.

INTERNET SITES

Home pages and directories will link you to a myriad of Web sites about
the ancient Mediterranean and Asian worlds:

Exploring Ancient World Cultures (University of Evansville):
  http://cedar.evansville.edu/~wcweb/wc101/
ArchNet (University of Connecticut):
  http://spirit.lib.uconn.edu/archaeology.html
ROMARCH, a home page on archaeology in Italy and the Roman
  provinces:
  http://personal-www.umich.edu/~pfoss/ROMARCH.html
The Ancient World Web:
  http://atlantic.evsc.virginia.edu/julia/AncientWorld.html

The sites you can visit include museums that specialize in the ancient
world, such as:

The Oriental Institute of The University of Chicago:
  http://www-oi.uchicago.edu/OI/default.html
Institute of Egyptian Art and Archeology:
  http://www.memphis.edu/egypt/main.html
Karanis (excavations in Egypt):
  http://classics.lsa.umich.edu/kelsey/OutKaranis.html

INDEX

Page numbers in *italics* refer to illustrations

Robert Green is a freelance writer who lives in New York City. He holds a B.A. in English literature from Boston University and is the author of *"Vive la France": The French Resistance during World War II* (Franklin Watts). He has also written biographies of three other important figures of the ancient world: *Alexander the Great, Herod the Great,* and *Tutankhamun.*